LEGAL NOTICE

The Publisher has strived to be as accurate and complete as possible in the creation of this report, notwithstanding the fact that he does not warrant or represent at any time that the contents within are accurate due to the rapidly changing nature of the Internet.

While all attempts have been made to verify information provided in this publication, the Publisher assumes no responsibility for errors, omissions, or contrary interpretation of the subject matter herein. Any perceived slights of specific persons, peoples, or organizations are unintentional.

In practical advice books, like anything else in life, there are no guarantees of income made. Readers are cautioned to reply on their own judgment about their individual circumstances to act accordingly.

This book is not intended for use as a source of legal, business, accounting or financial advice. All readers are advised to seek services of competent professionals in legal, business, accounting and finance fields.

You are encouraged to print this book for easy reading.

Introduction

In the United States, over the past few decades, if you were to look at the top ten prescribed medications in the country, anti-anxiety and antidepressant medications will always make the list.

This is not an accident, nor is it a fluke. We live in a very stressful world. In fact, a lot of Americans are struggling with anxiety disorders at some level or another.

It may have different manifestations, but make no mistake that it definitely gets in the way of a more effective life. Whether you want to be more successful in your relationships, or you just want to be a happier person, or you would like to be more effective in your career, you need to deal with anxiety.

Unfortunately, this is easier said than done because the vast majority of people cope with anxiety in all the wrong ways.

If you are reading this book, chances are, you are struggling with anxiety at some level or another, or you have a loved who is.

Please understand that this book teaches you alternatives that will help you overcome anxiety.

Ultimately, anxiety is a combination of your environment, your genetic predisposition, as well as your chosen coping mechanisms.

Never underestimate the amount of control that you have over your situation.

A lot of people are under the impression that if they have some sort of genetic predisposition for any kind of condition that they basically have no say in what afflicts them.

In other words, they really have no choice over their situation.

This really is too bad because the multi-billion-dollar pharmaceutical industry benefits when people continue to believe this.

Because if there is no individual control over anxiety and it's just a foregone conclusion, and your only choice is to go through some sort of counseling paired with psycho-pharmaceutical intervention, there is really not much you can do.

You really don't have much of a choice.

Well, please understand that you have a lot more control and say over the matter than you give yourself credit for.

Now, please understand that I'm not saying that you should not get professional help in terms of psychiatric or psychological guidance.

I'm not saying that at all.

I suggest that you work with a
professional, but please understand that
you can supplement whatever
they give you or prescribe to you with
things that you can do on your own.

These are mindset resetting strategies
that would enable you to retain control
over your life.

The reason why you're struggling with
anxiety is that, ultimately, you feel that
you're not in control.
You feel that you live in a world you
didn't create and, for a variety of
reasons, there is just something
bad that's about to happen or you're
struggling with guilt, remorse, doubt and
other negative emotions
about the past.

Well, please understand that the past is
the past. Those facts already happened.

It's not like you can jump into a time
machine and reverse what happened.
Those are facts.

They happened already.

There is really not much you can do about them.

That milk has been spilt.

By the same token, if you're worried about the future, there's really not much to worry about because
things haven't happened yet.

The things that you fear have yet to unfold.

The only choice that you really have is to deal with your mindset in the here and now.

The more you maximize your control over your present mindset, the better your relationship with your past becomes and the better equipped you would be to handle the future when it happens.

This book teaches you how to overcome anxiety without drugs, without professional and expensive psychiatric counseling, and by simply helping you rearrange your "mental and emotional furniture."

List Down All the Things that Cause You Anxiety

This assumes that you know what anxiety is and that you have certain feelings towards certain things in many areas of your life.

This is not always the case. A lot of people have undiagnosed anxiety.

They really can't quite put their finger on it, but whatever it is, it is upsetting them.

They won't label it as anxiety, but it may function like anxiety.

So, to the best of your ability, write down all the things that you are aware of that cause you anxiety.

Write Down All the Things that You Fear

Since a lot of people are unclear about what causes them anxiety or what anxiety exactly is, we're going to just go by a self-audit regimen that uses strong emotions or strong feelings as a guideline.

So, in this instance, you're going to list down all the things that you are afraid of.

List them all out.

There's no such thing as a wrong answer. If it seems irrational or almost cartoonish or funny, write them down anyway.
This is all about you. Nobody's going to read your answers.

The key here is to help you get a full picture of the things that weigh you down and hold you back.

List Down the Things that You are Guilty of

These are things that you are remorseful of.

These are the things that you wish didn't happen.

Maybe these are things that you did in the past or said in the past.

Write them all down.

There's really no intensity level here.

As long as you can remember it right now, and as long as it does come up in your mind from time to time, that's good enough to write down.

Write Down the Things that You are Doubtful of

Do you have relationships that you are doubtful of?

Maybe you feel like you don't love your parents?

Maybe you feel that your parents don't love you?

Maybe you feel that you don't really believe in the religion of your parents or the religion you've chosen, or you don't have much faith in your partner?

Whatever it is, write down the things that you're doubtful of.

Write Off the Top of Your Head
Be as spontaneous as possible.

here is no such thing as a right or wrong answer, so write down everything because we're trying to come up with a full audit of everything that's knocking around in your head.
As much as you can, try not to edit yourself. Remember, nobody's going to check your answers. What's important is that you get everything down that you are thinking about. As long as it enters your mind,
write it down.
Don't second guess yourself. Don't edit what you wrote down. Think clearly about what happened. And
as long as it enters your mind and as long as you can clearly describe it, write

it down as is.
Don't edit it. Don't tone it down or scale it up.

Give Yourself Time to Write Out Full Lists

If it takes a couple of days or even a week or two, that's okay. Just give yourself the time to write a completely exhaustive list of all the things that you are anxious about.
It's important to note that when you're doing this, you shouldn't put any stress on yourself. Don't think that this is some sort of deliberate, pre-planned, highly calculated exercise. That's defeating the purpose.
The whole point here is to come up with a massive list to audit your anxieties. For this to happen, you have to be as comprehensive as possible.
Unfortunately, when you put a lot of stress on yourself, you tend to edit yourself. You tend to highlight certain things and crowd out others.

The better approach is to go about writing all these things like you're in the shower. Remember the last
time you were in the shower and you came up with this idea? Well, people do that all the time.
Because when they are in the shower, they're not pushing themselves to think one way or the other.

They are more susceptible to genuine insight and flashes of intuition.

Do that when you are doing a self-audit.

Rank Your List in Terms of Intensity

Read your lists and rank them in terms of intensity.

When you think about, for example, the father you never knew because he abandoned you when you were still in your mother's womb or when you were a little kid, how do you feel about that?

How intense is the emotion?

What kind of emotions do you feel?

Do this for all the things that you have listed. This is going to take some time. It's easy to look at what you've written at face value.

It's very tempting to think that if you remember certain memories as being emotionally intensive, then that's that.

You might want to do things differently.

Give yourself the opportunity to really feel the emotion.

How intense is it?

Is it consistently high?

Are you sure this is not just a one-time thing?
Are you sure you're not remembering a memory?

Those can be quite tricky.

The emotions have to flash in your mind the moment you think about these memories.

You can't think about being angry in the past about that memory.

That doesn't work. It has to be a firsthand emotional experience.

Give Yourself Time to Adequately Gauge Intensity

Since you're going through each item and each has its own unique emotional impact on you, give yourself some time to do this.

Think through each item on the list.

Now that you have given yourself time to adequately gauge or appraise the intensity of the emotions of your memories, you need to take one extra step. This is a very important step. Avoid the tendency to read into the intensity of your emotions.

In plain English, this means that the emotions have to be intense in and of themselves.

The moment you think about something, intense emotions have to flash in your mind. That's how immediate it should be.

Avoid thinking about situations where you're thinking about something, and then the fact that you are thinking about it and you start feeling bad about the memory, and THEN it starts getting really intense.

The intense emotions you're feeling are not really about the memory itself, but the act of you going over the memory.

Do you see the difference?

One of these situations has something to do with the actual facts of the memory.

The other is just your interpretation of those facts.

Again, there's a big difference.

Be Completely Honest

Please understand that you're not trying to impress anybody here.

You're not trying to prove something.

You're not trying to be some sort of role model.

Nobody's watching.

Nobody's going to see your list, so it's extremely important that you be completely honest with yourself.

Because if you're not honest or if you somehow hold back, the only person that would suffer is you.

And ultimately, other people around you, namely your loved ones, will suffer as well.

So be completely honest about your prioritization and ranking of these anxieties.

Start Categorizing with Your Most Intense Anxieties

Starting with the anxieties that really get your goat, ask yourself where they relate to.

Can you come up with a broad theme that unites them?

Are they things that happened in the past? Are they things that involve some sort of abuse?

Are they things that you regret?

Are they things that involve people you blame for a lot of what's wrong in your life?

Are they things that you feel are part of your personal weaknesses that make you vulnerable?

Come up with other themes.

The key here to come up with a clear picture or a clear box for each list that you have.

And the more you go through your list, the more these patterns will emerge.

Categorize All Your Anxieties

This is going to take a while, but you need to categorize all the anxieties that you have listed based on the themes that you have detected.

I have to admit, coming up with categories for memories and emotions that you have can be quite confusing. This is why it's a good idea to feel free to mix and match different categories.

Please understand that there is no one perfect category that would fit most of your emotional experiences.

Just feel free to mix and match to come up with new categories that are more descriptive.

Feel free to do free association.

Don't automatically assume that since a lot of people think that a certain memory has to be categorized a specific way that that's the only way to go.

When you do free association, certain pairings might come up. You may be able to identify new categories that you didn't think of before.

You shouldn't feel any kind of pressure that you're just cramming all your memories or all your selfaudit data into just one box. This is the key. Don't feel that you're in any kind of pressure to do this.

Also, it will help tremendously if you get rid of "the right way" versus "the wrong way" mindset when classifying your emotional memories. Remember, they are yours. You have all the rights in the world to classify them in a way that makes sense to you. This is the key.

Because you're doing this to help yourself.

You're not doing this to impress other people.

You're not doing this because it's some sort of homework assignment that will be graded.

It has to make sense to you so you can help yourself with your anxiety issues.

Feel free to list the same anxiety among many different boxes.

Maybe it's something that happened in the past that you can't forget, and it's also a cause of regret, and it has also an abusive experience.

In that case, put that experience under three boxes.

Make Notations of the Intensity of the Anxieties that You have Categorized into Themes and Rank Them

To the best of your abilities, rank your anxieties within each of them.

This is not going to be easy because, oftentimes, when we remember a traumatic incident, it's as if we got hit by a tsunami. Our emotions just get the better of us and it seems so intense.

But when compared to the other anxieties that we have, and when we have a Big Picture perspective, it turns out that that anxiety that seems so strong and so overpowering is actually fairly tame.

So, you have to have a Big Picture perspective when ranking all these anxieties under each theme.

If You Believe, You Will Achieve

Please understand that belief is the cornerstone of your life.

If you believe, you will achieve. If you don't believe, it's going to be a much harder road for you.

This may not necessarily mean you would fail, but you're going to have a harder time.

You have to have your mind in the right place before you go on this journey of overcoming your anxiety. Otherwise, your mindset will sabotage you, undermine you, and constantly get in the way.

Before you know it, because of your mindset, you just run out of steam.

What's So Important About Your Mindset Anyway?

Your mindset dictates your life.

Mindset equals selective perception, selective analysis, selective response, selective action, which triggers elective reality.

How does mindset impact your reality?

Believe it or not, your mindset helps you edit your reality.

I know that's kind of a strong word because when you edit something, you change its form.

You change its direction. Eventually, you change its quality.

We all are editors of our own personal realities. Just because most of us don't step up to this responsibility and take full ownership of it, it doesn't make this fact go away. All of us have this capability.

This is how it works.

You have a mindset. Believe it or not, you have chosen it at some point in time.

It may not seem like it, but that's the way it is. It's chosen.

You're not going to hang on to your mindset if you didn't choose it.

This mindset is not neutral. When you take in all these objective stimuli from the rest of the world, you process them through your mindset and you give them meaning.

This is called analysis.

It may seem natural, it may seem like this is the objective reality, but don't kid yourself.

This is subjective because two people with two different mindsets can look at the same exact set of facts and walk away with two totally different conclusions.

That's the power of mindset.

Your childhood, your upbringing, how people treated you, any kind of abuse you suffered, what kind of beliefs you have – all of these impact your mindset.

And it's yours.

You process reality through the lenses of your mindset, and guess what happens?

That's right.

Your emotional state is affected.

This then leads to you responding to whatever is happening in a certain way.

When you respond, this is where the world kicks in.

How come?

Well, when you take an action, there are consequences.

For every action, there is a reaction. Reality works that way.

This is why, when you adopt a certain mindset, whether you're conscious about it or not, you eventually end up with a certain reality.

And it's all a choice.

Until and unless you take full ownership
of this, then you will continue to be the
person who keeps
asking "What happened?" instead of the
person who makes things happen.

Your Life is the Product of Your Mindset

You have to take responsibility of your
life. The fact that you are under a
tremendous amount of
anxiety and you're feeling guilty over
certain things or you feel ashamed of
certain things is because,
ultimately, of your choices.
Now, please understand that I'm not
blaming the victim here. Maybe
somebody did sexually abuse you,
maybe you were the victim of a crime,
maybe other people had it in for you and
did you harm, but
that's not the point.
The point is, how you responded to
those events is your responsibility
because the same traumatic thing

can happen to two totally different people, and they can have two totally different responses.
I know this is a simplification, but this is the truth.

Your mindset plays a big role in how you perceive the world's stimuli.

Your mindset plays a role in how you perceive and accept reality.

You have to take ownership of this.

You have to boldly proclaim, with no ambiguity, and with full honesty and sincerity, that you chose your life. Stop blaming others.

When You Blame Others, You Hand Them Power and Responsibility Over Your Life

When you blame other people for whatever has gone wrong in your life or, worse yet, your personal
failings, you are essentially giving them control over your life.

Think of it this way, if your father abandoning you as a child, or your mother abusing you when you were little, caused all your problems, who, ultimately, can fix them? This is not rocket science.

This should be pretty straightforward.

Let's put it this way, if you walked into a store and you broke something, who can make amends?

Who can put things back together?

Here's a hint: it's not the shopkeeper.

Do you see how this works?

Since other people that you continue to blame to this day "broke your life," then it logically follows that they are the only ones that can fix your life.

They broke it in the first place, so they can fix it.

Here's the problem. Those people are already living their lives or they're dead.

They're gone.

However you want to slice and dice it, they're out of your life.

They've moved on. Continuing to wait for them to make a cameo appearance back in your life to put things together is simply just setting yourself up for failure.

This is what happens when you blame other people.

You're constantly saying, "I'm not responsible because this person did that at that time" or "This situation happened to me."

Well, this is the most powerless thing you could ever do to yourself because you are putting the solution to whatever is wrong with your life in the hands of people or situations that you cannot control.

It's bad enough trying to change yourself, can you imagine trying to change other people?

Can you imagine trying to talk them into coming back into your life and repairing your life?

Fat chance.

They've moved on.

They've changed.

You have to take responsibility.

You have to take ownership.

You have to take the initiative.

I know it hurts because it's so unfair.

But guess what?

Life is unfair.

You have to make that step.

You have to take ownership of your life by saying, "It may not be my fault that this happened, but it is my responsibility to myself that I accept how I process this information."

In other words, you stop blaming others and you take full ownership and responsibility over what's going on with your life.

You have to Commit Yourself to Changing Your Mindset

If you change your mindset, everything that I'm going to discuss involving overcoming anxiety is possible and highly probable.

You would be well-equipped to do the emotional and psychological heavy lifting needed to effect profound change in the way you perceive reality, in the way you carry yourself, as well as how you get along with others.

In other words, you get a shot at living a new, more victorious life.

But it all begins with your decision to change your mindset.

How important are decisions?

You have to understand that there's a big difference between actually deciding and thinking about making a choice.

Too many people confuse the two.

They think that they're making a decision when what they're really
doing is that they are thinking about making a choice. They are not quite there yet.

They're still weighing a lot of things. They're still considering a wide range of factors.

But in their heads, they've already come to a decision.

This is why a lot of people who think they have a decision end up failing because they never decided.

When you decide, your mind is locked into a particular outcome.

You also line up your emotional state regarding a certain issue with your decision on that issue.

There's nothing wishy washy about this mental state.

You're locked in, and you have turned your motivation on.

You're pumped up about the decision.

Now, you may be thinking that all sorts of magical things happen after that decision point, assuming that you do reach a real point of decision.

I wish it were that simple.

Deciding is just the first step.

When you truly decide, then it means that you're going to follow up with commitment.

How important is this?

You know you're committed when you continue to put in the work and the time even though you don't feel like it.

You know you have fully committed when people around you are saying you're stupid or you've made a mistake and are telling you to turn back.

You know you've committed when you face one difficulty after another and all sorts of unforeseen events happen, and you still stick to it.

That is the power of commitment.

As awesome as that may be, that is only triggered once you have made a decision.

These two go hand in hand.

Changing Mindsets is Not Easy

We're all creatures of habit.

Even if we commit to change, sometimes our old habits and patterns kick in.

But you have to remain focused and dedicate your willpower to overcoming your habits.

Focus on what you stand to gain.

Focus on the relief that you get turning your back on the things that make you feel frustrated, sad, pathetic and angry now.

If focusing on what you stand to gain is too hard or seems to be too far off or abstract for you, do the opposite.

Focus on the pain of staying where you are and not changing.

You see, there are basically two kinds of people in this world.

On the one hand, there are people who are drawn to achievement and the better things in life.

In other words, they let their desires motivate them.

On the other end are people who will only lift a finger to change their circumstances when they feel
that they're about to lose everything.

In other words, they are motivated by fear.

Here is the good news: there is no right or wrong answer.

Whether you are motivated by your highest hopes, dreams and values or you are pushed by your fears and insecurities, it doesn't matter.

What matters is you put that foot right in front of the other, and you keep on walking towards that goal.

So, focus on what motivates you and make that change happen.

Dedicate Yourself to Mindset and Attitude Change

Set up a set of affirmations These are short statements you say to yourself non-verbally, but very clearly as many times as you can per day.

This might seem ridiculous, but affirmations work.

Why?

They function as conscious reprogramming of your personal narrative.

If you're struggling in any area of your life, it's because you have a personal narrative that makes that struggle happen.

For example, if you have a tough time honoring your commitments, you may be operating from a personal narrative that tells you that you're not a very trustworthy person or you're just too busy to commit.

You really can't keep your word because you have so many other things going.

Besides, deep down inside, you are a victim.

Affirmations work because they allow you to consciously come up with a new program or description for yourself.

The more you repeat this, the more likely it will sink in and become part of your conscious mindset.

It doesn't work overnight, but through focused and dedicated repetition.

Start a personal change diary Your personal change diary may seem like a simple ministerial task. After all, you're just making entries on your personal journey to transformative change.

At a certain level, it may seem like not much is happening.

It might even seem like you're just going through the motions or, worse yet, just wasting your time.

You should get these negative houghts out of your head because starting and keeping a personal change diary can truly change you as you work to hange your mindset so you are less anxious every single day.

How come?

Well, when you look at how you started and the mindset that you had as well as your description of your personal world and compare it to who you have become, you can't help but feel motivated.

Think about it this way, when you began this process, you probably thought that your anxiety and your
fears were basically who you are. You feel trapped.

You feel that there's just really no way you can get out of this situation because you're just stuck.

This is who you are.

This is ingrained in your essence as a person.

But when you look at a later entry and you notice that your mindset has changed, this gives you hope.

Things weren't as hopeless as you thought.

It turns out that things aren't as bleak as you originally imagined. This gives you a good reason to keep pushing forward.

Sure, the changes may not be all that dramatic, but there's no need to be a hero.

The fact that you have changed, even in the slightest degree, is good enough for you to draw hope from.

This enables you to recommit yourself.

Please remember, the key to transforming your mindset so you're less anxious and less fearful and more effective as a person is commitment.

The good news is that it doesn't take much for your sense of commitment to be encouraged.

It just needs a simple change.

Look for that change. Identify and track that change by starting and keeping a personal change diary.

Recommit yourself every day to this project of changing your mindset Celebrate the power of daily commitment The problem with a lot of people committing to certain changes in their lives is that they think that they are already committed.

After all, in their minds, they're thinking, "Well, I'm doing the same thing day after day, aren't I?

Isn't that commitment?"

To a certain degree, they are absolutely correct.

But to turbocharge that process and unleash the power of that daily decision to commit to a certain set of actions regardless of what are feeling and regardless of what's going on around us, a little bit of consciousness is required.

By simply saying to yourself "I am committing today," and then the next day saying the same thing and meaning it, you line up your conscious capabilities with your habitual side.

This gives you more power.

This also reawakens or reminds you of your sense of purpose.

Remember, you're trying to change your mindset.

You're trying to do something that is very difficult to do.

It usually takes a tremendous disaster for people to change their mindset or something unbelievably good.

Outside of those fairly rare circumstances, people stick to their mindset.

You're working on something grand.

Accordingly, you have to be as conscious about the process as possible so you can attack it with full power.

Challenge Your Mindset Every Day

Hanging out with difficult people is annoying and can seem like a waste of time.

But it can also be a tremendous opportunity to test whether you're making progress in changing your mindset.

Remember, you're not changing those people. That's not the point.

The point is whether the people who used to throw you off or upset you no longer do because that's the only way you would know if you are really making changes.

You can give yourself all sorts of affirmations and you can think of all sorts of warm and fuzzy images
about the change that you are trying to achieve, but until you actually pull it off in situations that normally emotionally challenge you, you're not really making progress.

So, find those challenges.

I know that most people would find these situations very difficult, even toxic, but that's precisely why you need to seek them out because they really push you to the limit.

You're not going to grow without pain.

You're not going to grow without challenges.

It's going to be very hard for you to change unless you put yourself in a situation where you're not comfortable.

List Down the Changes in Your Mindset

Have you stopped automatically blaming others?

Have you stopped automatically blaming yourself and feeling guilty?

Are you more proactive?

Are you more likely to assert yourself?

Are you more likely to speak your mind?

What changes do you see?

If you don't see enough changes, then challenge yourself more.

Put yourself in situations that would normally irritate you, hurt you emotionally, and see if you can withstand and overcome.

Remember, this is trial by fire.

Because baby steps are not going to cut it for most people. They hold
back and they stop growing.

You're going to have to commit yourself to this.

Victory is All About Consistency and Constancy

It doesn't really matter how many times you think you've failed.

What matters is that when you get knocked down, figuratively speaking, you spring back up.

Sure, it hurts the first time around and you probably want to linger on the floor, but eventually, you get
used to it. Eventually, you toughen up. And before you know it, you reach a point where you get knocked down and you spring back up.

That's called emotional grit.

That means that you will stick to your path no matter what. And that is a sign of maturity and progress.

Stop Letting Your Past Define You

Too many people let their past define them. They screwed up badly, and they think that their only value to humanity is their screw up.

They think that that's what defines them.

They think that they really can't progress past that point.

Maybe you went to jail.

Maybe you are accused of something.

Maybe you did something to somebody else that you regret.

Maybe you were abused and made to feel small, powerless and weak.

Whatever happened to you, please understand that it's the past.

The Past is the Past

The past is the past. You don't have a time machine that you can jump into and change the facts that happened.

Those facts happened.

Your job now is to live your life in such a way that you are happy, well-adjusted, effective, and loving and kind. In other words, your job is to live today.

Unfortunately, you're not doing that when you are worrying about the past and burning tremendous emotional energy thinking about what could have happened, what should have happened, or what would have happened.

The more you think about people who hurt you, the uglier they get, the more intense the pain becomes, and this poisons your relationships and mindset today.

You're not being responsible when you do that. You're not being in control when you do that.

Tackle the Past Head On

You have to resolve to tackle the past head on.

Every few days, you need to open up your diary or journal of past events, and then go through the process below.

You owe this to yourself. You have to be consistent about this for you to get out from under the weight of the past.

Ask Yourself if the Past Trauma that You Remember Really Happened

There is such a thing as false memory.

In fact, false memories are implanted all the time.

If you don't believe that false memories are possible, think back to the 1990s.

In the 1990s in the United States, there were all sorts of scandals involving therapists feeding false memories into the minds of their patients or clients.

This is due to the fact that human beings are very suggestible.

When you come across somebody who you trust and have confidence in primarily because of their title

or their supposed authority, you put yourself in a very vulnerable position. You put yourself in a position where they can easily influence you; where their suggestions can even seem like they came from you.

In the 1990s, a lot of counseling and psychiatric therapy sessions were kind of free form.

There weren't really clear protocols regarding suggestibility.

It is no surprise that in this climate, there were all sorts of false memories due to suggestions and false associations made in the minds of patients by therapists who highlighted or suggested certain associations.

Lives were broken.

Imagine growing up in a family where everybody loved each other and everybody got along.

You had a tremendous respect for your father and your mother.

And then later on in life, when you developed alcoholism or you had problems in your marriage, you see a therapist.

The therapist then leads you through a sloppy, unstructured process where you end up with false memories of abuse against your parents. How can you regain the relationship you have with your father when you had this false memory that he raped you as a kid?

Do you see how this is a problem in the 1990s and continues to be a problem today?

False memories are more prevalent than we assume. Be careful with them. Question all your memories.
The human memory is actually very faulty.

We often remember things by association.
When we come across somebody or an event that somehow gets associated with things that we
remember in the past, our memory gets jumbled up and we come up with a completely new story. It
turns out that what we thought was true is very far from it.
So, ask yourself, when you're looking through all these past traumatic events that you have prioritized
in your diary, did they really happen?
To the best of your memory, ask yourself, did they really happen? This means that you were there. You
heard something, you smelled something, you saw something, you touched something, or you tasted

something.
In other words, with your five senses, you could perceive that this was reality. If that's not the case, can other people corroborate that this did happen to you?

Do you know somebody who's close to you who could tell you, "Yes, that did happen.

I saw it with my own two eyes" or "I was there, I witnessed the whole thing" or "I heard her say that" or "I heard mom say that to you," and so on and so forth.

So, if you did not directly perceive it, ask if you can get evidentiary support from somebody else.

If not, then mark those experiences.

Eliminate False Experiences

If you can't find any documentary proof or if you don't have any personal remembrance of an event, and you can't find any corroboration from anybody else, decide, once and for all, that these events did not happen.

The next time you start to remember them, say to yourself in a bold voice, internally and silently, "This is false.

This is fake.

This is not a real memory.

I don't want to have anything to do with this."

When you do that, you shut down the normal wave or chain reaction of negative emotions that you feel.

Why waste tremendous amounts of emotional and psychological resources on things that did not happen?

It may seem artificial, it might even seem like you are basically just spitting in the ocean, and it's really pointless and futile, but you have to keep repeating the pattern above until it makes sense.

This is a key part of you taking full ownership over your false memories.

If you still aren't pumped up about this, just think about the misery you feel when you entertain false memories.

They make you feel small, they make you lose trust in people, and they make you feel weak.

It's not a good place to be.

Tie that bundle of negative emotional states together with the alternative to not repeating memory selfownership statements.

Sure, repeating these statements over and over again may seem boring, pointless and ineffective, but what else do you have?

You really can't say that what you have right now is going to be so much better.

In fact, the reason you're reading this book is because you want to get out from under all that anxiety, fear and negative emotions brought about by false memories.

There is misery in false memories, so focus on that.

Say to yourself, "Okay, this might seem repetitive, it might seem mechanical, deep down inside I feel like I'm just wasting my time, but what do I really have as an alternative?

Do I really want to go back to the misery that my false memories bring?"
When you paint things in such a stark way, that contrast highlights the value of what you're doing.

I know you probably have a million and one other things that you'd rather attend to. We're all busy.

But believe me, when you call out your false memories and you repeat these statements, you start reclaiming your life. This action is an investment in a better life.

This is Not Denial

Please understand that you are not practicing denial.

You're not sweeping an elephant under the rug.

Instead, you're being rational.

If you did not experience it, and nobody else around experienced it, then, for all practical purposes, it
didn't happen.

Why are you going to have to continue to beat yourself up about something that didn't happen?

This is fiction.

And for whatever reason, throughout the years, you hung on to that fiction.

Maybe it helped explain your situation, maybe it gave you a lot of excuses, maybe it served some sort of purpose in the past, but now it's a burden.

Now, it's holding you back and dragging you down from the kind of life you should be living.

It's time to end the madness and just constantly stop yourself when you remember that thing.

Once you start thinking about it, just say, "This is fake. I'm lying to myself when I do this."

Phrase your rejection in the worst way possible.

Maybe you should say, "I'm being a fool if I think about this because this is false memory.

This is not real. I'm going to stop being stupid." Something like that.

Eventually, you will get used to it and you will stop.

Because it doesn't make any sense to waste any more emotional resources on things that didn't happen.

Identify Your Exaggerated Memories

After you have identified and knocked out your false memories, the next step, after a few weeks or even a few months, is to focus on your xaggerated memories.

These are memories that actually happened.

People were there.

You yourself can vouch that this actually happened.

There is some sort of evidence that it happened.

Nobody can dispute that these things really happened.

But the problem is, you exaggerated the details.

In other words, you blew it out of proportion.

You overdramatized things.

So, something that could have happened to other people and they could just shrug it off or blow it off, you chose to hang on, blow it up, and attach a very toxic significance to it that it continues to bother you to this very day. These are exaggerated memories.

Relive Each Exaggerated Memory One by One

As much as you can, put yourself in a situation where that exaggerated memory occurred.

Put yourself in the scene.

Imagine yourself in that place.

Zero in on the facts as you know them.

These are just the facts, okay?

Not your interpretation.

Please understand that those are two totally different things. Focus on the facts as they happened.

Write Down Fact vs. Interpretation

Analyzing what happened to you, write down, to the best of your ability, what actually happened and what you think happened and what you think it ignified or what you think it meant.

Please understand that these are reactions.

These are interpretations.

Write a Long List of All Your Interpretations

Interpretations and personal analysis change over time. As we mature and as we change, our interpretations change. So just come up with a long laundry list.

Pick Out Interpretations that Empower You

There are many ways to interpret a situation. There are many ways to look at it.

Many are self-defeating. Many make you feel depressed, small, weak, and powerless.

Many feed into your personal narrative that you are some sort of victim.

Those are negative interpretations.

Of the long list of interpretations you have of that experience, pick the one that makes you feel empowered.

These are interpretations that make you feel like you're somebody, that you have some sort of control of your life, or that there is some sort of tomorrow. In other words, there is an out or an opportunity for hope. Those are positive interpretations.

Kill Your Negative Interpretations by Understanding Their Nature

Look through your negative interpretations of the past memories and just ask yourself,

"Am I overblowing these?

Am I just exaggerating them?

Am I just reading too much into these?

Because whatever it is that I am reading into of what happened to me, it's not helping me now.

This interpretation is not doing me any big favors." So, use this analysis to clean out your list of interpretations of events that actually happened.

What's left are empowering interpretations.

Play Up Your Empowering Interpretations

As long as your empowering interpretations are based on actual facts, you are not engaged in selfdeception, self-hypnosis, or any such thing. Instead, you are basing your interpretation on fact.

But you need to look at your positive interpretations and be clear about them.

Are they directly related to the experience?

Do they flow directly from the experience? If they do, then amplify them.

Because you have to understand that if you went through a negative experience, that can be a breakthrough moment.

Instead of something that can make you feel small, weak, powerless, ugly, repulsive, dumb, stupid, unwise, foolish, or whatever, you can use that experience as something that is a breakthrough to personal power, autonomy, strength, wisdom, beauty, transformation and hope. It's all about perspective.

But you have to base that transitional perspective from merely positive or

merely okay to very positive
on facts.
So, go back to the facts of those
experiences and say, for example, "My
father left my mother before I
was even born.

This experience enabled me to be a
more independent person, to be always
grateful for what I had, and to work hard
for everything that I have."

If this sounds familiar, this is the Lebron
James story.

Do yourself a big favor, look at what
happened, and look at the victory there
by looking at the positive impressions
that you have in making those shine.
Emphasize those.

**Test Your Change of Mindset by
Constantly Thinking of Exaggerated
Memories**

When you think of these exaggerated
memories, automatically focus on the
positivity.

Automatically focus on the sense of empowerment that you feel.

Eventually, it becomes a habit.

Because previously, when you think about these memories, you blew them out of proportion in a very negative way.

You felt crappy. You felt weak. You felt nasty.

Now, you feel good. But it's still the same basic facts.

But you have to understand that what doesn't kill you makes you stronger. Sure, it may seem devastating at that time, but it was actually the push that you needed.

For example, a girl that was told by her mother that she's ugly grows up to be a supermodel.

Why?

Because she wanted to prove her mother wrong.

She didn't have the luxury of everybody telling her she's beautiful, so she learned how to become more
confident based on other things that enhanced her natural beauty.

Let's get one thing clear.

There are all sorts of people in this world who will just have it in for you.

For whatever reason, you rub them the wrong way and they have resolved to make your life hell.

At the very least, they're going to tell you that they don't like you. Fair enough.

The truth is, just because other people say certain words or actions to harm you, it doesn't necessarily mean that they will harm you.

To paraphrase Eleanor Roosevelt, "Nobody in this world can make you feel lousy without your permission."

Whether you feel inferior, ugly, repulsive, dumb, flawed, scummy, shameful, it doesn't matter.

All of these are interpretations.

You don't have to accept their "gift."

You don't have to allow them to reach
you because ultimately, you
are in control.

Either you're in control or they're in
control.

Do you see the stark choice?

Take control.

Take ownership.

It may not be simple, it may not be easy,
it definitely may not be
comfortable, but it's absolutely crucial.

You have to Adopt Some sort of Mindfulness Practice to Change and Always be Aware of Your Mindset Mindfulness enables you to zero in on the present moment.

You're not bent out of shape about the past, and you're not weighed down by the anxiety of the future. Instead, you are focusing on what's happening right here, right now. You're focusing on reality as it unfolds.

Different Models of Mindfulness for Different People

Different people have different preferences as far as their mindsets are concerned.

Some people do well with certain types of meditation and mindfulness ractices, others do less as well.

The key is to avoid thinking that there is some sort of one-size-fits-all mindfulness solution for you.

Instead, cycle through and experiment with the different mindfulness options I'm going to give you below.

Please understand that this is not an exhaustive list.

There are many different variations to these, as well as many different unique ways of achieving mindfulness.

I'm just giving you these as a sampler. Once you get used to these echniques, or you pick one and it works for you, you might want to take
things to the next level and explore other

related mindfulness or meditation options.

Present Observation Meditation

This method is also known as "single object observation."

When you practice "present observation meditation," all you're doing is looking at an item in front of
you.

That's all you're doing.

What makes this type of meditation or mindfulness practice so powerful is because you pour all your sensory effort at that object.

When you're that focused on the texture, the color, the shape, and all other descriptive dimensions of
the object in front of you, you're not thinking about past childhood trauma.

You're not thinking about the things that you normally worry about.

You're definitely not feeling any anxiety.

Instead, you just allow your mind to focus all its power on something that exists in front of you, right here, right now.

This clues you in to the present moment and helps you establish a tremendous amount of mental, emotional and psychic discipline.

Awesome, right?

Waking Meditation

Also known as "walking meditation," this is one of the most practical meditation/mindfulness techniques available.

"Walking meditation" or "waking meditation" is all about allowing yourself to be fully present in an outdoor setting, taking in all the sights, sounds, smells, tastes and textures. In other words, you're allowing yourself the full opportunity to be fully alive in a particular point in time and in a particular place.

When you're taking in all this input, you allow yourself to get locked in the present moment and your mind is not wandering.

You're celebrating life and time within a tight space.

Sure, you're walking, but your point of focus walks with you.

This is a great way of taking full ownership of your surroundings mentally.

This builds a tremendous amount of discipline because you're constantly shifting your focus.

It also allows you to be out and about and commune with Mother Nature, but at your own terms.

So, this is a very powerful form of meditation exercise.

And it's also very practical. You're not locking yourself behind closed doors, you're not assuming the lotus position, and you're not even closing your eyes. Instead, you're out and about out there, completely living your life.

Transcendental Meditation

This technique uses a silent mantra.

"Transcendental meditation" has a scary ring to it because of the word "transcendental."

A lot of people are not all that comfortable with religion. It doesn't sit well with them.

I understand.

Fair enough.

But please remember that transcendental meditation uses a silent mantra that doesn't mean anything.

Mantra, in the Buddhist or in the Hindu tradition is supposed to mean something.

This is not one of those. It's just a repeated saying that enables you to

pace your breathing so you can track
your consciousness in a rhythmic way.

Transcendental meditation is powerful
precisely because it enables you to
create a consciousness rhythm within
you that empowers you to destroy
thought. Done right, transcendental
meditation doesn't trigger thought.

How powerful is that?

You're suffering from anxiety because it
seems that almost every other thought
you have is something
fearful, worrisome or horrific.

There's just something about each and
every passing thought that adds to
your fear of either the past, the future, or
your concerns about other people.

Transcendental meditation is the
complete opposite of that.

It is 180 degrees away from any notions
of self, fear, doubt, anger or emotions.

How come?

You don't think.

Thoughts are vaporized by transcendental meditation.

They can't even begin to bring some sort of emotional impact because they don't even materialize.

That's how powerful transcendental meditation is.

And the best part to all of this?

It's effortless.

You just repeat your silent mantra and eventually it sinks in.

Eventually, your thoughts start to vaporize sooner rather than later.

And before you know it, they don't even form.

Really mind-blowing stuff.

In fact, a lot of people report tingling in their extremities because they are freed from material and physical attachment and grasping.

There's no need to always feel in control.

There's no need to prove yourself.

There's no need to hang on.

That's how powerful transcendental meditation is.

Counting Your Breath

This technique enables you to watch your thoughts overhead.

When you count your breath, eventually, you will be able to achieve distance from your thoughts.

It's like you're sitting back and watching the clouds roll through the sky.

As big and as dark as certain clouds may be, if you look at them long enough, you would notice that they're slowly moving.

Eventually, with enough time, they will completely pass overhead.

When you learn how to count your
breath and acknowledge your thoughts,
eventually, they will just
simply pass over your head.

When you learn how to do breath
counting correctly, you would realize that
you only need to acknowledge your
thoughts.

You're not denying them.

You're not sweeping them under the rug.

You're just acknowledging that they
exist, and then you let them move on.

You don't take hold of them, you don't try
to reduce them into terms you could
understand, you don't try to conquer
them, you don't try to confront them –
you don't do any of that.

Those are the things that you normally
do, and that's why you're anxious.

That's why you are wracked with all
sorts of negative emotions like guilt,
remorse, and a sense of orthlessness.

Instead, when you count your breath, you still take ownership of the thought because you acknowledged that it's part of you, but you let it pass, only to be replaced by another thought.

And you let that pass.

Before you know it, you will start to be able to think about certain things without necessarily getting all worked up and emotional about them.

This, in and of itself, makes the counting of your breath mindfulness practice worth incorporating into your daily routine.

Regardless of which flavor of meditation or mindfulness you adopt, pick one.

You will do yourself a very big favor when it comes to managing your anxiety on a permanent and sustainable basis.

Unless You Feel It, It's Not Real

All of the stuff that I taught you here are worthless if you keep it in your head.

You have to act them out.

You have to put them into practice because then, you will get a reaction from the rest of the world.

The truth is, it doesn't really matter how the world reacts.

What matters is how you respond to their reaction.

That's how you know if you're maturing.

That's how you know if you're changing.

It is scary because now you're being proactive and you're not just lying down and taking what the world
dishes at you passively.

But you have to understand that the more you try, the better you get at it. You have to work with a sense of emotional urgency.

Overcoming your anxiety through changing how you process stimuli from the outside world and your
relationship with the past will produce amazing benefits.

If you're still unclear or you don't really get that nice surge of emotional urgency when you focus on
things you stand to gain, flip the script. Try to get emotional urgency from the fact that if you don't change the way you're doing things, you're going to get worse.

If you think things are bad now, wait until you let your anxiety get even worse.

Focus on the loss, the crippling doubt, the sense of powerlessness. Are these enough to push you to put one foot in front of the other as you make the journey to an anxiety-free life?

Unleash the Power of Momentum

When you do something repeatedly, you get better at it. You can take that to the bank.

That is not a theory.

That is not speculation.

That is reality.

Regardless of whether we're talking about trade, school, relationships, or whatnot, whenever you keep doing something over and over again, you get better at it.

You get to figure it out, you get to find out the nuances, and eventually, you get the hang of it and you become more successful at it. So just hang on to it.

Give Yourself a Nice Boost of Motivation

I have a secret for giving myself a nice boost; for motivating myself when I feel like I've run out of steam when I'm trying to change the way I look at the world and the way I deal with my anxieties and fears.

I just read my personal journey diary and I look at my first day and I compare what I was feeling and
thinking that day with what I'm feeling and thinking now. Believe me, this just gives me so much hope and fills me with so much motivation.

It reminds me that I made some progress.

I'm not a sad case who cannot change.

I can have hope in change.

So, do this.

And it doesn't matter whether you just started on Day One and then you're comparing the entry on Day
Five.

There is some sort of change.

You may have to look for it, it may be small, but that small change is a cause for hope.

Get an Ally

Humans are social animals. We do so much better when we are with other people.

We do so much better when we help other people.

Do yourself a big favor, get somebody to help you.

This is an ally.

It may be your girlfriend, your boyfriend, your spouse, or it could be your parent.

Whoever it is, it must be somebody who loves you.

That person is basically going to walk with you through your journey.

Let Your Ally Hold You to Account

The cornerstone of the system that I have taught you in this book is honesty and sincerity.

In other words, for you to overcome your negative mindset and negative self-programming, you have to be completely honest with yourself.

And unfortunately, it's very easy for us to lie to ourselves.

It's very easy for us to buy our own selfdelusions.

Well, you have to give permission to your ally to check you.

Basically, you have to give permission for them to hurt your feelings.
Because it hurts to be told that we're being self-delusional.

That whatever we're saying is not true. We're lying to ourselves.

That hurts to hear, but it's absolutely necessary.

So, give that person permission so that person can properly help you.

For a surgeon to heal, he must first cut.

Always Review Your Personal Narrative

Everybody has a narrative. Everybody has this hidden script that is the story of our lives that we tell ourselves.

We say to ourselves, "Oh, I'm poor" or "I'm dumb" or "I just can't do it" or "This is who I am."

Those kinds of things. Well, those are things that hold us back.
And it's really important for you to look at your personal script based on what you've learned about your mindset and your past, as well as your anxieties about the future.

Allow Yourself to Feel Good

When you've changed your mindset and you've started seeing changes, own up to it.

Say, "This is a good thing.

I'm making progress.

I have the right to be happy about this."

One of the most common and most frustrating things about anxiety is that you never allow yourself to feel happy.

You never allow yourself to feel that you are doing something right.

Well, if you notice a big change, and your ally tells you that there is a big change, celebrate it.

Take him or her out for lunch.

Think about what you've achieved. It's a milestone.

Because before, you were somebody different.

Now, you're one step closer to the person who you want to be.

The information that I've given you in this book is worthless if you don't put it to use.

You have to take action on these materials.

You have to take action today. You have to commit to it.

This is not one of those things that you can just get into, jump in with both feet, and then after a couple of weeks, give up.

This is a lifelong thing.

Because when you are more mindful about the things you choose to think about, you start thinking about the right things.

You start thinking about your life in such a way that you are able to feel happy, complete, and victorious.

Because eventually, things will fall into place because you feel more empowered.

This is the life you chose, not the life somebody imposed on you. Not the life that some random lottery put into your lap.

In other words, you start living an empowered and responsible life.

Worktool 1

CHEAT SHEET

How to Free Yourself From Anxiety

Step 1: Do a Self-Audit

- List Down All the Things that Cause You Anxiety
- Write Down All the Things that You Fear
- List Down the Things that You are Guilty of
- Write Down the Things that You are Doubtful of
- Write Off the Top of Your Head

Step 2: Prioritize Your List

- Rank Your List in Terms of Intensity
- Do this for all the things that you have listed.
- Take your time

Step 3: Categorize Your Anxiety Challenges

- Start Categorizing with Your Most Intense Anxieties
- Categorize All Your Anxieties
- Feel free to list the same anxiety among many different boxes.
- Make Notations of the Intensity of the Anxieties that You have Categorized into Themes and Rank Them

Step 4: Believe that You can Overcome

- If You Believe, You Will Achieve
- Remember: Your Life is the Product of Your Mindset

Step 5: Understand that The Future Begins with YOU

- You have to Commit Yourself to Changing Your Mindset
- Remember: Changing Mindsets is Not Easy Focus on what you stand to gain.
- Dedicate Yourself to Mindset and Attitude Change
- Set up a set of affirmations,
- Start a personal change diary,
- Recommit yourself every day to this project of changing your mindset.)
- Challenge Your Mindset Every Day
- List Down the Changes in Your Mindset
- Victory is All About Consistency and Constancy

Step 6: Take Hold of Your Past

- Stop Letting Your Past Define You
- Remember: The Past is the Past
- Tackle the Past Head On
- Ask Yourself if the Past Trauma that You Remember Really Happened
- Eliminate False Experiences

Step 7: Overcome Exaggerated Memories

- Identify Your Exaggerated Memories
- Relive Each Exaggerated Memory One by One
- Write Down Fact vs. Interpretation
- Pick Out Interpretations that Empower You

- Kill Your Negative Interpretations by Understanding Their Nature
- Play Up Your Empowering Interpretations

Step 8: Practice Mindfulness

- You have to Adopt Some sort of Mindfulness Practice to Change and Always be Aware of Your Mindset
- Present Observation Meditation
- Waking Meditation
- Transcendental Meditation
- Counting Your Breath / (Watching your thoughts overhead.)

Step 9: Practice, Practice, Practice

- Unless You Feel It, It's Not Real
- Get that sense of Emotional Urgency
- Unleash the Power of Momentum
- Give Yourself a Nice Boost of Motivation

Step 10: Adopt some Best Practices for All-Natural, SelfDirected Anxiety Solutions

- Get an Ally
- Let Your Ally Hold You to Account
- Always Review Your Personal Narrative
- Allow Yourself to Feel Good

Overcoming Anxiety
How to Stop Struggling and Start Living
MINDMAP

Do a Self-Audit

List Down All the Things that Cause You Anxiety
Write Down All the Things that You Fear
List Down the Things that You are Guilty of
Write Down the Things that You are Doubtful of
Write Off the Top of Your Head
Don't edit yourself
Give Yourself Time to Write Out Full Lists

Prioritize Your List

Rank Your List in Terms of Intensity
Give Yourself Time to Adequately Gauge Intensity
Be Completely Honest

Categorize Your Anxiety Challenges

Start Categorizing with Your Most Intense Anxieties
Categorize All Your Anxieties
Make Notations of the Intensity of the Anxieties that
You have Categorized into Themes and
Rank Them

Believe that You can Overcome

If You Believe, You Will Achieve
Belief is the cornerstone of your life.
Your Life is the Product of Your Mindset
When You Blame Others, You Hand Them Power and
Responsibility Over Your Life

The Future Begins with Y-O-U

You have to Commit Yourself to Changing Your
Mindset
Changing Mindsets is Not Easy
Dedicate Yourself to Mindset and Attitude Change
Set up a set of affirmations
Start a personal change diary
Recommit yourself every day to this project of
changing your mindset
Challenge Your Mindset Every Day
List Down the Changes in Your Mindset
Victory is All About Consistency and Constancy

Taking Hold of the Past
Stop Letting Your Past Define You
The Past is the Past
Tackle the Past Head On
Eliminate False Experiences
This is Not Denial
Overcoming Exaggerated Memories

Identify Your Exaggerated Memories
Relive Each Exaggerated Memory One by One
Write Down Fact vs. Interpretation
Write a Long List of All Your Interpretations
Pick Out Interpretations that Empower You
Kill Your Negative Interpretations by Understanding
Their Nature
Play Up Your Empowering Interpretations

Practice Mindfulness

You have to Adopt Some sort of Mindfulness Practice
to Change and Always be Aware of Your

Mindset
Different Models of Mindfulness for Different People
Present Observation Meditation
Waking Meditation
Transcendental Meditation
Counting Your Breath / Watching your thoughts overhead

Practice Makes Perfect

Unless You Feel It, It's Not Real
Unleash the Power of Momentum
Give Yourself a Nice Boost of Motivation

Adopt Best Practices for All-Natural, Self-Directed Anxiety Solutions

Get an Ally
Let Your Ally Hold You to Account
Always Review Your Personal Narrative
Allow Yourself to Feel Good

Overcoming Anxiety
How to Stop Struggling and Start Living

RESOURCE REPORT

RESOURCE SHEET

Self-Audit Resources

List of things that cause you anxiety (general)
List of things that cause you anxiety (specific)
List of things you FEAR
List of things you DOUBT
List of things you feel GUILTY about

Quality Checklist
- write off the top of your head
- don't edit your list
- don't explain, just list
- give yourself enough time to write out a long list

Audit List Ranking Checklist

Read your lists and rank them in terms of intensity
- are the emotions intense?
- are your emotions clear?
- do they trigger vivid memories?
If you answered YES to all 3 above, rank the emory higher.

Best practices
- Give yourself a long time
- Be Completely Honest

Categorize Your Anxiety Challenges

List by intensity
Vibrancy of memories
Your tendency to 'lose it' when gripped by these thoughts
Simple 'categorization tricks' that will help you draw associations and connect the dots
- mix and match to see patterns

- free association
- don't judge your associations in terms of right vs wrong

Do a belief self-audit

- what do you believe about your identity
- what do you believe about your capabilities
- what do you believe about your skill sets
- what do you believe about your path in life
- what do you believe about your parents
- what do you believe about your job / career / boss
- what do you believe about your relationships

What do your beliefs tell you?
- your power
- your ability to make things happen
- your ability to forgive
- your ability to start over again

Pick out beliefs that empower you

- Start with the outcome
- Trace back to the current mindset YOU NEED TO HAVE to achieve
positive outcomes